LOVED
BACK
to
LIFE

~ HOPE IN YOUR BROKENNESS ~

SEYI JENYO

Loved Back to Life:
Hope in Your Brokenness

Published in the USA

ISBN 10: 978-1533613523
ISBN 13: 1533613524

✝

This book is dedicated to the One who loved me back to life, God, my Abba Father! Thank You for loving me beyond description, thank You for taking my broken pieces and making me Your masterpiece. Thank You for Your light that shone upon me even in my darkest days, thank You for being there for me even when I didn't know it, thank You that when I lost hope and was stuck in the pit of my mess, Your hands were waiting for me to hold on to, to bring me out. Thank You that when the enemy thought he had me, You kept a hedge of your protection around me, kept me alive and brought me through. Thank You Lord that Your love for me never grew less when I lost faith in You. Thank You for healing and restoring me. And finally, thank You for pouring Your love into my heart, that I may experience love, know love and give love and hope to others.

CONTENTS

ACKNOWLEDGEMENT

I would like to use this opportunity to thank the woman I call my mother, who raised me and loved me just like her own. Thank you for always believing in me and encouraging me.

I would like to thank my very close friends who have supported me in the journey I have been on in the last 2 years. Without you all, the journey would have been harder than it already was. Thank you for always praying for me, encouraging me, believing in me even when I didn't, pushing me to Christ and always loving me for who I am. You ladies are more than a blessing to me and words will never be enough to express my gratitude.

Thanks to everyone who has helped with making this book possible, the editing, formatting, book cover, the support, encouragement and prayers. I appreciate you all.

Last but not least, I would like to give it up to my Heavenly Father who turned my tests and tribulations into my testimony and gave me the privilege to write this book to encourage someone out there.

INTRODUCTION

Could life get any worse than it already was? This was the thought she woke up with most mornings, stuck in this pool of everything bad you could think of, darkness inside and out, negativity oozing from every breath she took, but still managed to play the "life is so perfect, I'm so happy" game so well. With this constant fight going on, on the inside, she knew deep down that there must be something better; though it seemed so far away from her reality.

As much as her life displayed the opposite of what she had desired and dreamt of, she always told herself she would not die and be a statistic. She would affirm herself saying "I am an anomaly, I know there is something I have to give, something special to offer the world, one day I will prove people and statistics wrong". This constant battle of dealing with her reality and fighting for this future she dreamt and desired for left her tired. Her current reality seemed to take over her dreams and get the best of her until she no longer knew who she was and what she wanted to be, which all got buried under life circumstances and the effects of it.

Overwhelmed, exhausted, anxious, defeated, lost, hopeless and dead were the best ways to describe this young girl.

Love was what she was yearning for, she wanted to be loved so desperately but nothing seemed to fill that void, trying to fit into the status quota of what she thought was expected of her to buy this ticket that will give her the love she was looking for. A young girl who just wanted to be accepted for who she was no matter what it would cost her, only to find all her tactics, decisions and actions were exhausted. Stuck in a pit dug so deep because life just didn't play fair, there was no difference between day and night as her life seemed like it was in permanent darkness.

Emotionally and mentally wrecked, dysfunction became the norm and it was time to say enough is enough. With the blow and punches life circumstances and situations gave, it left the conditions of her heart with a flat line as it would be displayed on an ECG machine struggling to keep going, but with the little strength, breath and faith she had left on the inside she still dared to hope; dared to hope that one day her life will get better, one day she would be loved and everything would be just fine! Though this future seemed so

far-fetched, the reality of this scripture rang true many years
later;

> "But hope which is seen is not hope, for how can one
> hope for what he already sees? But If we hope for
> what is still unseen by us, we wait for it with patience
> and composure" (Romans 8:24-25, NKJV).

That young girl was me! The love I was desperately seeking
was something I could not find in the world, until I gave my
life to Christ. I came to understand the true definition of
what love is and Who love really is. 1 Corinthians 13: 4-8
perfectly describes what love is:

> "Love endures with patience and serenity, love is
> kind and thoughtful, and is not jealous or envious;
> love does not brag and is not proud or arrogant. It is
> not rude; it is not self-seeking, it is not provoked [nor
> overly sensitive and easily angered]; it does not take
> into account a wrong endured. It does not rejoice at
> injustice, but rejoices with the truth [when right and
> truth prevail]. Love bears all things [regardless of
> what comes], believes all things [looking for the best

in each one], hopes all things [remaining steadfast during difficult times], and endures all things [without weakening]. Love never fails [it never fades nor ends"] (AMP).

God is love!

In this book, I will be sharing my journey of being **LOVED BACK TO LIFE**. It is a testimony of God's unconditional love, His mercy and His grace. I pray that you are encouraged to hope, reminded that there is a love so real and true, one that can bind up your wounds. I hope that you understand that in the hands of God, you are never too broken to fix. He took all my broken pieces and made me His masterpiece. What the enemy meant for bad He turned it all around for my good and in the grand scheme of things I was accepted, loved beyond description, my identity was restored, I was given hope, I was healed, delivered, set free and made whole! If God did this for me, He is more than able to do the same for you too.

CHAPTER 1

REJECTED TO ACCEPTED

How Rejection Affected Me

Rejection is one of the root causes to many issues, insecurities and problems that a lot of people face. Unfortunately, many do not recognise that it is not a product of how they behave or respond to things but it is the root, the reason why they do what they do. A lot of the things I have dealt with or had problems with stemmed from the root of rejection and I didn't even know it.

Rejection stinks…that's right, it stinks! It is not hard to know those who suffer from rejection, well I definitely know because deep recognises deep. I carried this odour around pretty much most of my life and it got to a point that even the perfume I wore could no longer hide the smell.

> *A lot of problems people face have stemmed from the root of rejection*

→ reminds me of woman w/ perfume (bible)

Many of us have been rejected from the womb; I was one of these people. My mum got pregnant and the man she got pregnant for left her to marry another woman. Rejected from before I was born gave me the false message that I was a mistake. I wasn't supposed to happen and that's why my dad didn't want to have anything to do with me. With my mum being rejected, I believe that was the first seed of rejection that got planted in me even before I was born. You may be thinking how do I know that? Well according to research, a mother's emotions can affect her unborn child. Babies tend to feel the way their mother feels; if you ever notice when a mother is sad her baby picks up her emotions quickly and knows she is sad and the same goes for when the mother is happy. So in terms of rejection, what the mother feels, so will the baby. And that is how I know I felt rejected from the womb, when my mother felt rejected from the father of her unborn child.

Being a mistake was something I concluded very early in my teenage years; especially when I came to the realisation that my mum got pregnant and my father left her. It made it seem like I was something that should have never happened, particularly because I didn't even know who my father was until after my mother died. So I believed the lie that I should not have been born, because the way I was conceived seemed like an accident. Questions I continually asked myself were; *why did my dad leave my mum for someone else? Why do I not know my father? Am I or my mother not good enough for him?*

The word 'bastard', was what I used to refer to myself often because one, I didn't know my father and two, it was what one of my step fathers always called me as a child when he had an argument with my birth mum. That word stuck with me till I grew much older. Clearly, calling myself this word made me have a low self-worth and self-esteem, I didn't think I was worth anything and so my expectation from other people pretty much was the same. But something deep down always wished I was worth more than I thought about myself.

Being adopted into the family I was brought up in was such a blessing, but had many challenges and difficulties I had to face. I have the privilege of being the eldest sibling to 2 brothers and a sister, in addition to my two brothers from my birth mother. So altogether, I have 5 siblings. My adopted family became my family more than my biological family, which I don't know too well. To no surprise, I was certainly different in many ways physically, so as a young child it became an insecurity I struggled with. I compared myself subconsciously and dealt with the battle of people saying we look nothing alike when they'd met or seen my brothers and sister. I would panic and hope in my mind that they wouldn't ask any more questions because being adopted was a big secret for me, nobody knew except those who were present in my life shortly after I lost my birth mother. I would constantly think and tell myself that I wasn't skinny or good looking enough. Even with my cousins from my adopted family, though we got on really well it became more apparent that I was the odd one out and this was a big and constant struggle for me till late in my teens. Even though I felt like the odd one out, I still wanted to be noticed in a good way, so I found comfort in doing the house chores, domestic things in the house, studying, writing, drawing and listening to music which eventually got me noticed, especially in regards to my school work as I always had extremely good results. My adopted dad made it quite clear he didn't like me but I never understood why; he made growing up very difficult and hard for me which made me feel even more rejected, which once again had a negative effect on my self-esteem.

Rejection and Character

Rejection can play a big part in your character, which brings about a false sense of identity because you begin to believe that it is just the way you are. Yes, it's easy to believe this because the effects of rejection make you respond and react the way you do every time you are dealing with one thing or the other.

Another way rejection can give you a false sense of identity is by what society defines as the norm. When you have been rejected you are more likely to want to fit into anything and everything just because you crave to be accepted. If society says one thing, it becomes your ultimate goal to conform to this particular thing or trend. Other times rejection can make you feel like you do not fit the part; so some people will shy away from society norms and feel rejected automatically. Their self-esteem and self-worth is low, they refuse to accept themselves for who they are and therefore disregard themselves. Sometimes, it's a case that you are not rejected, but because of how you think, you have already jumped to the conclusion that you have been rejected which then makes you act in ways that will later have you rejected.

There were certain characteristics I had that stemmed from the root of rejection.

Possessive: I was quite possessive, if I had something I found it hard to let go. I will be honest, this even applied in relationships and at times friendships. If it really meant a lot to me, I would not allow anyone or anything to take that person from me, even if it was not a good relationship. I was very sly in how I portrayed this which made me quite manipulative at times. This is not good because it's very similar to a jezebel spirit (controlling). Every now and then I sometimes struggle with this, but thank God He is continually working on me and changing me. Before it was something I couldn't help doing but now that I'm on this journey of doing things the right way; Gods way… I am able to recognise when the signs of possessive behaviour start to show in my relationships. What I do now is pray and give it to God to help me to be generous, sharing and trusting.

Rejection can cause you to be possessive because of the fear of losing someone that means so much to you to someone else, but acceptance allows you to be free to know that if the person is really for you they will not leave you and can still be your friend even with having other friends too; especially if it is a relationship that has been ordained by God (which I had to learn in order to enjoy the relationships God has blessed me with).

Anxiety, worry and overthinking: Many times in my life, I made sure I didn't offend anyone and if I felt like I did, I would go out of my way to make sure they knew I was sorry. To an extent, I wouldn't see this as a bad thing because it is not necessarily nice going around hurting people and thinking you can just get away with it and not say sorry. But the problem is you end up always walking on eggshells, not being able to be yourself. At the end of the day, no one is perfect and there are days where we can act out of character, but what I used to do was make sure I was in everyone's good books. If I felt like I wasn't in someone's good books, I began to worry and overthink things. Most of the time it was usually nothing deep but yet in my mind I had magnified the issue which could easily have been resolved in a short conversation. The danger with this was that I would end up in self-condemnation. Even after it had been resolved, I would still beat myself up because of what I did and ensure I never repeated it. Once again, I wouldn't see this as a bad thing because it's important to acknowledge our mistakes as individuals and learn from them, but one must move on, which is what I struggled doing. Not only did this steal my peace of mind, but it kept me in real bondage; bondage to people. Wanting to be liked, loved and approved was like my life depended on it, but as God dealt with rejection in me, He made me realise the reality of the matter was that people will fail me. So the reliance on their love, like, approval and acceptance was certainly not something I would want to be dependent on otherwise it would become an avenue for disappointment, bitterness, hurt and the very thing I didn't want...REJECTION. I learnt this as I gave all these flaws to God to deal with and now I know the only place I get my approval from is God and that should be the same for you too.

Overdoing: Giving too much of myself too quickly was something I had no control over at times, thinking about it now it makes me cringe because I'm thinking gosh Seyi why were you so needy?? This became very apparent when I started dating guys in college. I only started talking to guys when I started college, so to be honest I didn't really know this was going to be an issue. As I reflected on why this was an issue, I was reminded that coming from a background where domestic violence and emotional abuse were a regular occurrence in the home, I didn't want that to be the case when I got into a relationship. I thought the answer to that would be to give the person what I think they want so that they would like me and not hurt or reject me.

Fear: Rejection played a part in many types of fears I had always struggled with; fear of failure, disappointment, people, rejection and death, to name a few. This caused a lot of limitation to what I aspired to do, but thank God for His love and patience, He made me understand I have no reason to fear but plenty of reasons to have faith. Thank God I am still a work in progress, so I believe it can only get better for me and for you who fears if you just believe God's words and promises for your life.

Chapter 1: Rejected to accepted

So in the same way hurt people hurt other people... it's safe to say rejected people reject people, some unknowingly, knowingly or both. I will use myself as an example - I did both. Knowingly I found it hard to accept people's love because I always questioned their motive, *were they genuine or not?* I would ask myself, *are they going to stay if they find out the real me?* So getting close to people took a while. However, on the flip side, if I liked someone or had a good vibe about them I could let them in easily and let too much out to gain their approval. This was more prevalent in relationships with the opposite sex. This became more evident when I was much older when I was in college and university. I gave too much of myself away because I wanted love, something the other person most likely wasn't ready for. I then became a burden because I was putting all my emotional needs on them. Though I was very good at hiding this, I believe I was quite manipulative emotionally. I wouldn't give too much away with words but I guess I showed how much I cared for the person by doing things I wouldn't necessarily do, but did it just to make the person happy in the hope that they would give me the love I was yearning for. What I didn't know was that this can push someone away. They could not fill the void that I wanted filling and it was only when I gave my life to Christ that I realised there was nobody or nothing that could fill that void but Him.

Here are a list of characters and signs that stem from rejection, many of these I used to relate to and some I have noticed in other people who suffer from rejection, I call them *REJECTION DETECTORS:*

- ❖ Possessiveness
- ❖ Over doer
- ❖ Insecurity
- ❖ Low self - esteem
- ❖ People pleaser
- ❖ Fear of man (people)
- ❖ Care too much about people's opinions
- ❖ Willingness to compromise and lower standards
- ❖ Living a double life (pretending to be what you're not)
- ❖ Fear
- ❖ Forceful relationships
- ❖ Manipulative
- ❖ Lack of true identity
- ❖ Always comparing self to others
- ❖ Desperate

- ❖ Easily offended
- ❖ Stand-off ish
- ❖ Bitter
- ❖ Angry
- ❖ Easily taken advantage of
- ❖ No boundaries

Hopeless to Hopeful

Having dealt with all the things mentioned previously, I had to get to a place of exchanging the lie of me being rejected with the truth that I am accepted. The Lord took me through the process of firstly renewing my mind and changing my perspective of how I saw and felt about myself. The very insecurities I didn't want to own up to, I had to be honest with myself and deal with each one as I was led to deal with them.

I am not a bastard because my biological father is still around and even if he is not active in my life, I have a God who is my Father, who has promised to never leave nor forsake me.

I am not a mistake but I was predestined to come into this world. God had a purpose and still has a purpose for my life so even though the way I was conceived might have looked like a mistake to the eyes of the world, God had a plan for the conception long before it happened.

Though I always felt like the odd one out growing up, though I didn't feel beautiful, was insecure and my self-esteem and self-worth were practically non-existent, the Lord started to show me that I am one of a kind and that I am unique. So I had to embrace my uniqueness and love being me. His word says that I am wonderfully and fearfully made and my inner self [soul] should know this (Psalm 139:14, [brackets mine], KJV (1st part) & AMP (2nd Part)) - today I believe just that.

I don't have to overdo things to be loved because God loves me unconditionally. I shouldn't try to earn love by doing for others, but rather I should do things in love freely but also have boundaries and be led by Him in all things.

I don't have to prove my self-worth or who I am to people to be loved because God thinks I am good enough and He loves me the way I am. I had to learn that it's either you like me for who I am or you don't; I can be free to be me without having to conform to the ways I think I need to be to be accepted.

The good news is that you and I are already accepted. Ephesians 1:4-6 says;

> *"According as He hath chosen us in Him before the foundation of the world, that we should be holy and without blame before Him in love; having predestined us unto the adoption of children by Jesus Christ to Himself, according to the good pleasure of His will, to the praise of the glory of His grace, wherein He hath made us accepted in the beloved".*

How amazing is that? God has chosen, adopted and accepted you and I; I don't think it can get any better than that. Why should we be craving acceptance from humans when we are already accepted by God? Knowing and getting the revelation of this truth helps to break the spirit of rejection and uproot the seeds of rejection.

Where does the rejection in me come from. Is it fuctional?

Seyi Jenyo

This was one of the things I had to realise, I had to exchange the lie that rejection fed me and substitute it for the truth that I belong somewhere and most importantly to someone and that is God. I no longer have to fear or worry about being rejected and abandoned again because God's word says He will take care of me, He will never leave nor forsake me, even if my mother and my father do (Psalm 27:10). That goes for you too, we have been adopted into the family of God hence why we are able to cry out Abba Father!

Jesus the Chief Cornerstone

> "The stone which the builders rejected has become the chief cornerstone, this is from the Lord and is His doing; it is marvellous in our eyes" (Psalm 118:22-23, AMP)

Dealing with rejection, God made it known to me that Jesus was and is the Chief cornerstone because He was rejected. Yes! Jesus the Son of God, He also was rejected by many on this earth so He understands the pain and hurt that comes from rejection, but He shows the flipside of what

> **The stone which the builders rejected has become the chief cornerstone**

rejection can do. In reality the enemy has used rejection in the lives of many to be a stumbling block, but Jesus has set a great example in how to deal with rejection. Despite all they did to Jesus He still loved them; He didn't allow anger, hurt, bitterness, fear or any of the nasty stuff that comes from rejection to affect Him.

So if Jesus is the Chief cornerstone, what is the cornerstone? According to the Oxford Dictionary, this has two definitions:

1. *It is an important quality or feature on which a particular thing depends or is based.*
2. *A stone that forms the base of a corner of a building, joining two walls.*

From my understanding this is a very important part of a building; the cornerstone is usually the largest and most solid part of a building, it is the first set stone that is laid and all other stones are set in reference to that particular stone which will therefore determine the outcome and structure of the entire building. So basically, without the

There is purpose in your rejection

cornerstone, there is no building or should I say there is no strong and secure building. In other words, there is purpose in your rejection! How? I hear you ask, well Romans 8:28 says;

> "and we know all things work together for good to them that love God and are the called according to His purpose".

There was and there is still purpose in Jesus being the Chief cornerstone why? Because Jesus is the foundation of the Church (Body of Christ), everything we do is built on Him. The right, solid and secure foundation!! Ephesians 2:20-21 makes this clear;

> "having been built on the foundation of the apostles and prophets, Jesus Christ Himself being the chief cornerstone, in whom the whole building, being fitted

together, grows into a holy temple in the Lord,"
(NKJV)

Peter boldly mentions this again in Acts 4:11;

"This [Jesus] is the stone which was despised and rejected by you, the builders, but which has become the Head of the corner [cornerstone]". (AMPC)

And this was precious in God's sight;

"Come to Him [then, to that] Living Stone which men tried and threw away, but which is chosen [and] precious in God's sight". (1 Peter 2:4, AMPC)

So imagine this is me and you who has been rejected, when God has seen this, the Bible says we should come to Him, let Him show us the purpose in that rejection we have had to deal with. In the process of showing us, we begin to know who we are in Him which then pleases Him and we are able to use the very rejection for something positive just like Jesus did.

So being rejected isn't all bad because if you allow the Lord to do a work in you, the results of that will be to declare Gods glory, and He will use you to make a difference in people's lives from your own personal experience. Being rejected can make it difficult to show love, but when you are able to accept God's love, rejection will need to be dealt with in order for you to pour out the love you have received from Him. This love you receive will help others who have been in similar situations to accept the love of God that is available to them and they can then do the same to others. This creates a domino effect where one person has allowed the Lord to deal with their rejection and heal them from it; it has a knock on effect on those that are ministered to through them. Jesus is the prime example, in Him being rejected He laid the right foundation, so we are to follow that and keep building on Christ by reaching out to others and helping them do the same.

When I got the revelation and the realisation that Jesus understood my pain and He was willing to take that away from me, I no longer had to carry the burdens and baggage of what came with rejection. I didn't have to make the effects of rejection become my identity, I didn't have to carry on walking around with 'rejected' written all over my heart and forehead, I didn't have to live a life bound to rejection because that makes me bound to people and Jesus wants me to be free. And that goes for you too. We are not to be bound to anything or anyone. Rejection has the ability to make us rotten internally, it alters the way we see ourselves, it alters our mind-set, which then affects our character and how we relate to people. So cry out to God to heal you, tell Him to show you the areas of your life that rejection has affected you and pray for the grace to endure the process He will put you through to overcome this.

Amen! apt

The word of God says that we are accepted in the beloved, we belong to the family of Christ through adoption (Ephesians 1:4-6). As human beings, naturally we yearn to be loved and cared for, but unfortunately the things we go through in life does the exact opposite which then tries to obstruct the natural sense of accepting and giving love. God pours His love into our hearts through the Holy Ghost (Romans 5:5) and He loves us unconditionally. You and I don't have to do anything to earn His love, He loves you and I despite our past, He loves us the way we are. Nothing, not

even rejection, can separate us fr
8:35-39). God is Love. That is who He

Prayer:

Father, thank You that You have the ability to take away the stink of rejection, thank You that You are more than able to uproot every seed of rejection and plant new seeds of Your love and acceptance. Thank You for allowing Jesus to be the Chief cornerstone where my life can be built on a solid and secure foundation, thank You that there is purpose in my rejection, help me to overcome the effects that rejection has had on me and help me to live a transformed life that You have destined for me. Amen!

CHAPTER 2

PERFECT LOVE CASTS OUT FEAR

One of the effects of rejection is fear. The spirit of fear tried to cripple me in many ways and areas of my life. When I started to take my walk with Christ seriously, He began to do an extensive work in me.

Don't let fear paralyse you

There was so many things wrong with me and the issues of life got the best of me but the reality of God's truth came alive in my life. 2 Corinthians 5:17 says;

> *"Therefore if any man be in Christ, he is a new creature: old things are passed away; behold, all things are become new."*

The Amplified Version breaks this verse down further;

> *"Therefore if any person is [ingrafted] in Christ (the*
> *Messiah) he is a new creation (a new creation*
> *altogether); the old [previous moral and spiritual*
> *condition] has passed away. Behold, the fresh and*
> *new has come!" (AMPC)*

This means my old life that has passed away includes the fear that was a part of it and it is time to embrace the new.

As much as this was good news for me, fear didn't just disappear overnight or the day I confessed Jesus as my Lord and Saviour. It was a process. I had to endure with renewing my mind daily, pulling down strongholds and holding thoughts captive as well as living out the truth of God's word.

In order to really deal with fear as a whole, I had to first identify that it was a spirit of fear and it was not just a part of me. I had to look at what areas of my life fear had dominated and then give them to God to help me overcome them one by one, and honestly when I look back, I realise that I was walking around scared of pretty much everything.

Being so hurt, rejected, abandoned, taken advantage of and bitter, I found it hard to believe that true love existed, so as much as I wanted to be loved for real, it was something I struggled to accept and embrace. I was so scared of real love because I didn't know what to expect from it, something inside me knew there had to be something better than the kind of love that I thought existed, but the fear of the unknown made it hard to comprehend a love that could be so real and perfect.

Some of my fears included the following; fear of failure, disappointment, rejection, someone loving me fully because I didn't know if it was genuine, fear of being transparent, fear of people's thoughts towards me and their opinions, fear of someone helping me as I never wanted to be a burden to anyone, fear of being noticed, fear of being the centre of attention, fear of animals, fear of the future, fear of relationships/marriage and the fear of premature death. I will elaborate on a few of them and the effects they had on me.

Fear of disappointment: I used to wonder where this came from for a long time, until during my journey of healing, the

Lord was showing me the roots of many issues I was dealing with and the fear of disappointment came from two things. I felt disappointed by God as a little girl when I prayed for my mum to get better but she didn't, and also from people I thought would be there for me in my time of need and didn't show up. So I found it hard to ask for help and learnt to do life all by myself. This caused a problem when I gave my life to Christ as I struggled to fully trust, rely and depend on Him. I found it hard to believe that He would not disappoint me again but as God continually showed me His love, my heart was able to get to a place where I could feel vulnerable and helpless deeply knowing that His strength is made perfect in my weakness and He will never forsake me.

Fear of relationship: As mentioned briefly in the previous chapter, I had a lot of issues and negative perceptions of family and marriage. I saw men as cheats, liars and harmful because that was all I ever knew and witnessed growing up at home. There was a desire in my heart for a family where love was very evident amongst everyone. I fantasised about a marriage that didn't have violence or abuse but just love, I would get lost in my thoughts imagining what the perfect marriage and family would look like but come back to reality knowing that it just didn't exist.

Growing up I always told myself I would never let a man treat me like crap, I won't let them treat me how my mothers were treated. Unfortunately, the very thing I didn't want to experience with guys I ended up experiencing just that. Because I was already desperate for love, I ended up trying to find it in the wrong places. I got taken advantage of, I got violated and worst of all, I got seriously mentally and emotionally abused. Being molested and sexually abused by my adopted dad was the final straw with taking any nonsense from the opposite sex which brought about homosexual tendencies. I started to see men as objects to fulfil sexual desires and I felt more drawn to women because they were the only people I knew showed me some sort of love and care. As wrong as I knew this was I just couldn't help it, so this was an issue I struggled with for many years, I would tell myself I was not a lesbian but my feelings would say otherwise. I started to get attracted to women and have feelings for them but still fight it at the same time because I knew this was not right. As much as I never wanted to admit it, I knew it was a constant struggle in my mind. Being called a lesbian when I was 14 in the playground by a bully shook something on the inside of me because back then, you dare not say that out loud. I felt so humiliated, violated and ashamed of being called that in public with a group of girls laughing at me. From that day I started to entertain those thoughts; *am I really a lesbian?* I would ask myself because to be honest I did have feelings towards girls, I just didn't understand why. Then I wondered whether I was bisexual because I was attracted to both male and females, as I literally saw men as objects to get sexual desires fulfilled and women as people who will love and show me affection without hurting me. This brought about a fear of relationships as a whole, but only in Christ was I able to be changed and transformed in my mind where I am now able to see that relationships, family and marriage are a blessing. My perspective was changed as I began the journey of healing and the Lord restored my identity and showed me that I love because He loved me first and the love I was yearning and craving for in both men and women could only be found in Him (1 John 4:19).

Fear of premature death: Losing my mother to cancer at the age of 8, invited another type of fear that continuously left me paranoid. I had almost accepted the fact that I would die at a young age and leave my children when they are not even old enough to know me. I thought maybe I had been cursed because my mum was the first born and so was I. I would have nasty thoughts of me being terminally ill or having an accident. This was a problem because I was not able to enjoy my present life because I was busy worrying about a future I may or may not see. Even though I will never fully understand why my mum died, I came to terms with what happened and that everything happens for a reason, whether I understand it or not and God is still sovereign. When I got to that place of understanding God's sovereignty, I was able to accept the reality that my future is secure in Christ no matter what happens, after all the thoughts of God towards me were and are good, not evil, to give me a future and hope (Jeremiah 29:11).

Fear of being noticed: The thought of speaking in front of people frightened me. I was crippled by what I thought their opinions were of me. I cared too much about what their thoughts were towards me. Even if they hadn't said anything, I could read what they are thinking by their facial expression and body language; I hated the thought of being the centre of attention. When people would compliment me, for example, "Aww Seyi you are beautiful", I would start feeling on edge, and I would get nervous especially if it was a compliment that was said in the midst of other people. In my mind I would think, *"Ah great now everyone is going to look at me"*. Instead of just saying a simple thank you and keeping it moving, fear once again made me act like such a drama queen in my mind. It was only when I started to see myself the way God sees me that I was able to embrace myself and accept compliments genuinely.

Fear of being transparent: I was ashamed of my life; I didn't want people to know the real me. I thought my life was too messy and complicated to even say the least. I just thought I was a weird person with so many problems. I was already fearful of people's opinions of me so why would I now go and shoot myself in the foot by being "real"? This was why I was so good at hiding my emotions and not sharing my problems with people, well the ones I trusted enough anyway. This affected me emotionally and mentally because I would be dealing with an issue or feeling some type of way for a while, but I'd rather let the thing kill me than for me to tell someone. Little did I know that was me being prideful because humility will scream and seek for help but pride will pretend that everything is ok so that your reputation won't be tainted; which is wrong. It not only gives a wrong perception of who you are but it has the capability of destroying you. It's just like having symptoms of a disease and you do not take yourself to the doctors or hospital, what happens then? The signs of the disease will start to become more obvious, you end up being really ill and in a worst case scenario you end up on life support or even dead. Which one is better? I think that's easy to figure out.

I am thankful that through my journey of healing and restoration this is something the Lord broke off me, I am able to embrace the real me whether you like it or not. Transparency, I have now learnt, is a beautiful thing. Having the freedom to be you is a breath of fresh air, being able to express yourself in time of need is very beneficial to your whole being (spirit, mind and soul) and in order to enjoy the fruits of love, transparency will have to be

Having the freedom to be you is a breath of fresh air

involved. In order to have an intimate relationship with God, transparency is key, even though He knows all things, He wants us to be transparent and be real with Him. He doesn't want a relationship with the fake you, He wants a relationship with the real you. The same goes with friendships and relationships as a whole; if you are not transparent how can people be real with you and vice versa; how can you stay accountable or be accountable to another? Now you can see the importance of transparency, this is why the enemy wants us to be silent so that we can be bound to whatever we are struggling with; but no more. Speak out and reach out to those you trust, be real and enjoy the freedom that comes with it. I am thankful to be delivered from this fear in particular because if this was not the case I would not be writing **Loved Back to Life**. Glory be to God!

I had a dream sometime in 2015, which made it clear how bound I was to fear. In the dream, I was running away from something and all of sudden because of how fearful I was, I started to lose control of my legs and my arms. I couldn't run any faster than I already was, I couldn't speak and I started to float in the air. When I managed to hold on to a tree nearby to keep me on the floor and stable, the tree came out of the ground, was floating in the air too and at this point I had lost all control over my body and felt useless. I woke up thinking what the heck was that dream about? I prayed and asked the Lord to make the dream clear to me. As I made breakfast before going to work, I heard so clearly the Lord say, *"Don't let fear paralyse you"* and He gave me a flashback of that dream. I was like wowwww!!! Fear can do that??? You may be thinking the same and I'm here to confirm with you that yes it can, just like it did to me in the dream, it rendered me useless. When you look at the definition of paralysis; the Oxford Dictionary provides one of its definitions as the *"inability to act or function properly"*. This is what fear can do, it can stop you from living out your purpose the way you're supposed to. So many of us are crippled with fear, but there is hope; you no longer have to be a slave to fear.

Hopeless to Hopeful

The same way Jesus can heal us from sickness, He can also deliver us from fear. Faith has truth attached all over while fear has lies attached all over.

> *"There is no fear in love [dread does not exist], but full-grown (complete, perfect) love turns fear out of doors and expels every trace of terror! For fear brings with it the thought of punishment, and [so] he who is afraid has not reached the full maturity of love [is not yet grown into love's complete perfection]"* 1John 4:18 (AMPC)

I was very intentional about getting rid of fear in my life, it had been something that controlled me for most of my life and I was tired of fighting this battle on my own. As the Lord took me through the journey of healing and restoration, this was a big part of the process; dealing and

Faith has truth attached all over while fear has lies attached all over

removing fear. When I came across this scripture above, especially the amplified version, I began to weep like someone had died. I cried out to God when I realised that in Him there is no fear, I wanted to know more of Him and it drew me closer to Him. I found the secret of overcoming fear and that was in Him, He gave me the key and I unlocked the door and walked into a life that was free from fear. It's in that place He helped me to renew my mind, He made me change my perspective, He made me see things from His point of view, He allowed me to recognise the tactics of the enemy when he tries to use fear to cripple me, He gave me confidence that I can overcome fear in Him. This is available for you too if you press in and come to know the One who takes away all fears. There are times that some of the things I feared will try and get the best of me, but now I respond differently rather than it consuming me, it makes me draw closer to God because once again in Him there is no fear. When I got the personal revelation of 1 John 4:18 for my life, my prayer changed from, *"Lord take away all fear"*, and it became, *"Lord perfect me in Your love so much so that there is no way fear can reside in me."*

"For God did not give us a spirit of timidity (of cowardice, of craven and cringing and fawning fear), but [He has given us a spirit] of power and of love and of calm and well-balanced mind and discipline and self-control" (2 Timothy 1:7 AMPC).

So if God has not given me the spirit of fear, who else would have given me this?? It's pretty obvious who. The devil, yeah the father of all lies! And what is fear? It is a lie, because everything fear does counteracts the truth; it takes away what is supposed to be a blessing and makes it almost come across like a curse. As I have heard people say before, fear is **F**alse **E**vidence **A**ppearing **R**eal - which is true!

Fear is the opposite of faith. In fear you believe the wrong things which brings about negative results and faith (faith in God) brings about positive results. When Jesus performed miracles and healings in the Gospels, faith was a key element to making these acts evident. Many times Jesus made reference to faith, He said, "Your faith has made you well", "Faith as small as a mustard seed can move mountains", "O ye of little faith", "Great is your faith", "Truly

I say to you, if you have faith", faith this faith that. It pleases God when we have faith (Hebrews 11:6) so that means it displeases Him when we have fear; thank God for His mercy, kindness and love that bears with us when we are fearful because this is not His heart for us; many times in His Word He tells us not to fear. He knows how crippling and limiting fear makes His people hence why we must allow love (God) to perfect us in Him; we must abide in Him so that fear does not take over us.

In Mark 9:24, the father of the epileptic son struggled with believing for his son's healing. He cried out "Lord please help my unbelief" (my weakness of faith), he was transparent about it and we should be the same, we should cry out to God to help our unbelief i.e. fear so that we can have faith instead. Clearly, we can see how important faith is, yet many of us suffer from fear. Can you see the devil's plans in making many of us fearful?? To ensure that we do not receive what God has for us, so that we don't live the life that has been predestined for us to live effectively and purposefully. So today, have faith and believe so that fear has no more hold on you and you will yield positive results (A life free from fear).

When you are in Christ, you are no longer a slave to fear, Romans 8:15 says;

> *"For [the Spirit which] you have now received [is] not a spirit of slavery to put you once more in bondage to fear, but you have received the Spirit of adoption [the Spirit producing sonship] in [the bliss of] which we cry, Abba Father!" (AMPC)*

How comforting is that?? When you are in Christ, being bound to fear shouldn't even be an option because He has given something far better; the spirit of adoption. In other words, from the spirit of adoption we have an inheritance and things we are entitled to and receive; fear isn't part of that list. So why do we entertain fear in our lives if we are one of Abba Fathers' own? It is time to fight for what is rightfully ours and fight to get rid of what isn't ours...one of them being fear! You can do this because in Him you have the victory, amen!

There are still areas of my life where fear can get the best of me at times but I am constantly reminded that the Lord has not given me the spirit of fear, I am no longer a slave to fear and there is no fear in love because perfect love casts out fear. So what are you fearful about? Let me encourage you to remember these truths, just cry out to Him and seek Him always. Psalm 34:10 makes it known to us that when we seek God, He hears us and He will deliver us from all our fears not just one, but ALL.

Prayer:

Father God, thank You that I no longer have to live bound to fear, thank You that in You there is no fear, perfect me in Your love daily so that no fear can reside in me. Highlight all the areas of my life where there is fear, the ones I know and the ones that I do not know and give me the ability to face and overcome them. Help me to endure the process that is required for me to overcome these fears and give me the grace to continuously seek Your face so that I am delivered from all my fears in Jesus' name. Amen!

CHAPTER 3

LOVE COVERS A MULTITUDE OF SINS

Forgiveness

When you've been hurt so much, people and life have done you many wrongs, it's an easy access point for bitterness, anger, unforgiveness, resentment and strife to make home in your heart. Yes, some of us, if not many, can say the things they have been through can never be justified and one must pay back every wrong that has been done to them, but what do you gain from that? Revenge? I can guarantee you that if it is revenge you want done, it may feel nice for a short while but what happens to the effects of what people have done to you now? You may have gained revenge but you still have anger, you may have gotten even with them but you still have bitterness, you may have seen "karma" take place but you still have strife and unforgiveness. So tell me, is it worth getting all that and you still remain broken? Well I don't think it's worth it if you're still left a mess.

The good news here is that there is a way to get rid of all the bitterness, anger, unforgiveness and strife that the issues of life may have caused and that is love. Yes, love is a weapon, your weapon and it certainly was and still is my weapon.

In my life, I didn't necessary want to revenge in a nasty way but I wanted to prove all the people who tried to make my life a living hell wrong, those who contributed to my suffering, those who were determined to destroy my destiny

Let love be your weapon

and those who were just used by the enemy to try and wipe me out. So I was determined in my heart that I would prove them all wrong, I would make it and be successful, I would show them that they lost this battle, bearing in mind that all this time I was not in Christ, I was just a girl who wanted to make it. To my surprise, how I planned my life certainly didn't go that way, I made many mistakes and learnt a lot along the way in the process of "trying to make it". When I gave my life to Christ, clearly I still had this same mentality initially, but it wasn't long until God had to deal with me. How I planned my life would only dig a deeper hole into my already messy inside. He has now shown me that He is a just God, and that I don't need to prove anything to anybody, but instead my life will be all for His glory and He will show me how that will be.

My personal revelation of God the Father is Love. I had to really get to that place of accepting God's love for me in order for me to love myself and others. Well to no surprises, the initial progress of allowing me to love was to deal with unforgiveness, bitterness, resentment, anger and strife. Love and all those things cannot dwell together. If we go back to what love is according to 1 Corinthians 13, we see that one of the qualities of true love is that;

"it is not touchy or fretful or resentful; it takes no account of the evil done to it [it pays no attention to a suffered wrong]" (Verse 5b AMP);

To me this means that love keeps no records of wrong doings. So in order to love the way God wants us to love, we need to learn to live a life where we do not keep records of wrongs.

In the 4 years I've been in Christ, this was one of the first things I had to surrender. I had to forgive! I remember that night in my small room in Cambridge, November 2012 crying so much and saying Lord I forgive this person and that person and mentioned every person's name that had caused me pain and whatever else they did, I laid it down and released them. I can't describe what happened in words fully, but I felt the peace of God consume me, I felt so much lighter; I didn't realise how much of a heavy burden I had carried for those 23 years of my life until that night. I slept so peacefully that night and I was filled with so much joy that I actually prayed for all of those people when I woke up the next morning.

A few months later into the following year, my biological father found me on Facebook and sent me a long message. At this point I was thinking could this really be my dad? I barely knew him as I only met him shortly after my mother died and had to go and live with him for a little while. Whilst I was there, I was physically and emotionally abused by his wife and his mother in-law for months. I had lost so much weight, I was not well looked after and I was scared I would end up dead so I requested to leave because I could no longer bare it. My father had not been in contact since I left. 15 years later I got this message in my inbox and my heart felt like it was about to come out of my chest, I was scared and didn't know what to do. I ignored the message for a few days and he messaged me again and I literally realised that this was a test from God; He wanted to see if I had really forgiven everybody that had caused me pain, including my biological father. This was just one incident where the Lord checked my heart to see if I was truly genuine, but also ensuring all unforgiveness came out completely. There were many more incidents after this that tested my heart and even though it was hard at the time, I'm thankful I passed the tests. I am now free from what people have done to me, I don't need to prove anything to anyone, God has chosen how my life will give glory to Him and that is by love. Revenge isn't for me to do, it's not about me at the end of the day but about how God is going to use my life to benefit others. So I rest in what Exodus 14:14 says;

> *"The Lord will fight for you, and you shall hold your peace and remain at rest."* (AMP)

So if you are still struggling with unforgiveness, remember that vengeance is God's not yours. Give it all to Him and release those who have caused you pain and you will see a difference in your life.

Forgiving others was one thing to come to terms with, but something I really struggled with was forgiving myself. After getting to a point where I was tired of being good and getting nothing from it, I decided to taste what the rebel life was about, so from the age of 17 I went wild. I joined bad company and I got involved in many activities I should have not been involved in, drinking, smoking weed (I didn't even like it, I just did it to fit in), not going to college and meeting up with boys seemed to be my idea of fun. Starting university, I tasted more freedom and went even wilder, but in a very subtle way. I was surrounded by things and a lifestyle that were not "Kosha" and once again I got involved in nasty things. Clubbing became something I loved doing, especially because I loved Afrobeats, and those were the days it was popping and me and my friends were well known for repping the Afrobeat sets by getting down and showing them how it's done. I lost my virginity at 19 to a guy I only knew for a few months, who I thought cared for me. I "loved" him because he complimented my body shape, always told me how good I looked, he lusted after me and I loved the attention! We both loved Afrobeats and very similar things, he was good looking, to me he was just the perfect guy in my eyes but as you would already know, I was a girl suffering from rejection who wanted love at all cost which unfortunately cost me my virginity and dignity. To make this worse, he made me do a lot of things I'm not proud of over the course of the two years we were "linking", only to find out he had a girlfriend all along - all this made me very angry with him and myself amongst other things.

I got into another relationship with a guy who was very overprotective of me (which was something I wasn't used to so that got my attention). He was sweet with words and after the previous guy, I thought this would be a rebound sort of situation, but I ended up falling for him and things got further than I thought it would. We were seeing each other for pretty much the rest of my university life. He ended up living with me, which made matters worse eventually, and it only went downhill from there and yet again I did a lot of things in the relationship I'm not proud of. Though the two guys I was with never defined our relationships, I was in a relationship with them in my head so I gave them anything and everything to make them happy and for them to love me. I was taken advantage of and was mentally and emotionally abused which really affected me. Forgiving myself was tough because I felt so ashamed, guilty and repulsed about the things I had done in those few years. I was so hard on myself and I didn't understand why God would forgive me, I felt like a mess and so dirty! However, when I got the revelation of Jesus' blood having the ability to wash us clean, if we walk in the light as He is in the light (1 John 1:7), I realised that included my past and every bad thing I'd done. If God could forgive me, who was I not to forgive myself? If Jesus died for the forgiveness of mine, yours and other people's sins who are we not to forgive? This really humbled me because me not forgiving is basically saying that Jesus' death was a waste of time... God forbid! When I got this revelation, I repented wholeheartedly and asked the Lord to help me forgive not just others but myself too.

Hopeless to Hopeful

The by-products of unforgiveness is bitterness, anger, resentment and strife, these are all silent killers because they eat you up on the inside without your permission. All you have to do is allow unforgiveness in your heart and then the by-products go ahead and causes destruction whichever way they feel they want to. Letting go completely is the only way you can move forward, so letting go of all those by-products only allows you to enjoy freedom at the level you're supposed to. Many think they are free yet they are harbouring unforgiveness and that is not true freedom. You may be free in other areas, but God wants you to be free in all areas of your life because whom the Son sets free is free indeed (John 8:36).

As I mentioned earlier, love is my weapon and it can be yours too. 1 Peter 4:8 (AMPC) says;

> *"Above all things have intense and unfailing love for one another, for love covers a multitude of sins [forgives and disregards the offenses of others]"*

Proverbs 10:12 (AMPC) also says;

> *"hatred stirs up contentions [strife], but love covers all transgressions". [Brackets mine]*

When you love, it has the power to extinguish the wrongs people have done and it makes you see them in a different way... God's way. Though whatever they may have done may have hurt, it's your choice whether you will allow that to affect you or not. It's either you let it get to

> **When you love, it has the power to extinguish the wrongs people have done**

you or you just love and not allow it to go any further to cause damage or open the door to the by-products of unforgiveness in your heart. You save yourself from grief by attacking back with love. I know it's easier said than done but clearly it works otherwise God wouldn't command us to do so. Think about it this way; none of us are perfect, we do many things that are wrong; it doesn't matter if it's not murder, it could be something as simple as lying but in the eye of God sin is sin and yet His mercies are new every morning, He still loves us the same. Jesus also told us to forgive always, He said seventy times seven times we should forgive daily, which means all the time. I don't think anyone can offend you that many times in a day anyway, so basically we just need to live a life of forgiveness and extend mercies to others just as God does to us. At the end of the day, you will be doing yourself more of a favour than them... you remain free and not bound. So cheers to a life of true freedom!

We are reminded in Ephesians 4:31 –32;

> *"Let all bitterness, and wrath, and anger, and clamour, and evil speaking be put away from you, with all malice; and ye be kind one to another, tender hearted, forgiving one another, even as God for Christ's sake hath forgiven you."*

You do your part in forgiving others and yourself and let God take care of the rest. After all, He is a just God and the Righteous Judge. Time to let go and move forward; greater things are ahead of you so don't allow this to stop you from reaching what is awaiting you.

Prayer:

God I thank You that because Jesus died on the cross, all my sins have been forgiven. Help me to forgive others and myself, just like You have done for me and help me to extend love and mercy to others just like You do to me always. Help me to not keep records of any wrongs, help me not to harbour bitterness, anger, strife and resentment in my heart but to love hard and always. Amen!

CHAPTER 4

THE REAL ME UNVEILED

Identity Restored

If there is one thing I have learnt on this journey of healing, restoration and wholeness; it is the importance of knowing who you really are. If you don't know your identity, then it's almost pointless living... a bit extreme right? But that is just the fact. Without your identity, you cannot live a life of purpose; our identity is the foundation to everything that makes us who we are and what we do. This is why when we have been through so much in our lives, the circumstances and situations we have had to deal with shake the foundation of who we are causing our identity to get buried so deep down that the very things we've been through start to define who we are.

Growing up, I felt like I couldn't be Seyi. After the death of my mother and all the drama that came with this circumstance, I felt like everything that took place after defined who I was. Being adopted was something I never told anybody about, the only people who were aware were those that knew my birth mother. In school, I painted this image of me as a girl from a perfect family, and life was good, but this was all a lie. I couldn't embrace the real me for pretty much most of my life, it was a constant struggle to just be me. I always felt like I was betraying my family I was adopted into if I ever said the truth about my life. I felt guilty and ashamed of my life so it was easier to just say nothing. Normally, a child may misbehave in one way or another and will get corrected and disciplined appropriately, but in my case it wasn't just that. My adopted dad always accused me of going around telling people that they were not my parents and told me that I was an ungrateful child because they took me in when no one did. This caused a lot of pain for me because I was constantly being falsely accused for what I didn't do or say. I felt like I couldn't be a normal child as I would be so cautious about not offending my parents. It was the main reason I ensured I was a good kid and teenager. I lived my life trying to please them in any way just to say thank you; after all I didn't have a million pounds to pay them to say how grateful I was; however, I would go above and beyond to ensure they saw good in me and I avoided the dreaded words of being ungrateful.

I was 18 years old when I had first openly disclosed a part of my life no one really knew. It was to a few of my really close friends at the time. I was at a point of just being tired of living a fake life and living a lie. It made it easier for me to share my heart when I would feel down as I was very used to writing my emotions and feelings on a piece of paper in the form of a song, rap or poem, but there was a difference in vocalising this. I believe this was the beginning of me embracing the real Seyi, but this Seyi was so broken; identity was still something I struggled with. Suffering rejection, abandonment, abuse, hurt, pain, bitterness, resentment, anger, strife as well as struggling with fear, low self-esteem, suicidal thoughts and depression basically defined who I was and buried under all those things was the real me that I couldn't find. Instead, I lived a life conformed to the standards of others so that I could feel approved and validated, so unfortunately that was what my identity was based on.

It was only when I gave my life to Christ that the real me was eventually unveiled. As I went through the process of letting things go and allowing the Lord to do a work in me, many layers were removed and the very person I was already on the inside begun to emerge. It had just been buried so deep that the real me was so hard to find and almost seemed non-existent. The constant battle of embracing who I am became easier to win each time I passed through the process of healing and restoration. It's on this journey of becoming whole that the unveiling took place, it was in this place that my identity was restored and my purpose was uncovered.

Your identity is the very core and foundation of who you are. When this is missing, there is a big problem. The reason why people are in such a mess is because of their lack of identity. If society isn't defining who they are; people or their circumstances are. This is why we have so many living a crippled life, many are living so broken and

> **Your identity is the very core and foundation of who you are**

have become so comfortable in their dysfunction. They

have accepted this as who they are and there is no hope for anything better than that... Well let me tell you; that is a lie. There is hope, hope in Jesus Christ.

Hopeless to Hopeful

Looking back at the girl I was to the woman I have now become, it's almost impossible to recognise myself. The difference is so evident that it's hard to believe. There is no psychology, counselling, therapy,

> **There is no psychology, counselling, therapy, medicine or theory that can bring about this change and transformation; it's not something that happens by natural causes but supernaturally**

medicine or theory that can bring about this change and transformation; it's not something that happens by natural causes but supernaturally. Doesn't this just show how amazing and real God is? Only He would go to the depth of your mess and pick you out of the dark pit you've been stuck in for so long and bring you out with His mighty right hand. He doesn't just stop there too, He loves you out of that mess, takes everything away that isn't you, brings out the real you whilst healing and restoring you at the same time. This process is not an easy one, it's painful but it is so so so worth it!

In order to find the real you, an internal work is mandatory and that is what God does. He starts from inside, He deals with the surface things and goes deeper and deeper as you endure the process. I know the things that God has been doing in me in the past 12 months is something He couldn't do 2 years ago, I just wouldn't have been able to cope, but thank God for His patience. His desire for us is to know our identity and that identity is in Christ Jesus. That is the foundation, the right foundation that the core of our being should be built upon, whether you agree with me or not. When our identity is secured in Christ, all the lies that we have believed and lived have to go, why? So that you can embrace the truth of who you are in Christ. Look at 1 Peter 2:9, it says;

"But ye are a chosen generation, a royal priesthood,
a holy nation, a peculiar people; that ye should shew

forth the praises of him who hath called you out of darkness into His marvellous light".

From this scripture, we can see that we are chosen, so we don't need approval from people to be accepted because we have already been chosen by God; we are royalty; so our worth isn't found in riches, or in relationships or anything we put our worth in. To be royalty is to be held in high esteem, so why do many of us suffer from low esteem when in the eyes of God, He thinks so highly us? We are to be holy; this is God's desire for His people,

> **You are chosen, you are royalty, you are holy, you are peculiar**

to live a life free from sin, but the very things we are struggling with automatically draw us closer to sin and make us desperate for love at all cost just because we are busy trying to find validation and fill a void that can only be filled by God. We are peculiar, meaning we are different; we are unique so why do we compare ourselves always? Why do we want to be like other people? We have been set apart for God's pleasure and purpose and we will not be able to embrace the real person we are if we are busy trying to be what we are not. We have been called out from darkness into His marvellous light, meaning clearly God doesn't want us to live in darkness; He is calling people out of that so they can see the light and actually see who they are in Him... The same way you can't see anything in a room that is pitch black, is the same way you can't see who you are when in darkness, but once the light comes on you see everything. Well, the same applies to when you are in His marvellous light, you can see the real you, which should reflect Christ hence why He does a work in you so you are able to see this.

In Genesis 1:27, God created mankind in His own image, so He knows who we are more than we know. In the process of restoring our identity, He wants us to see ourselves as He sees us. When He finished creating man, He said it was *good*, meaning that our identity should only reflect what is good. If it doesn't, then it isn't of God! He is constantly moulding us and perfecting us in order for us to look how He originally intended. So what am I trying to say here? I am saying it's not too late and God wants to restore your identity. The enemy has allowed life and circumstances to invite struggles that will taint the very person we are. The enemy comes to steal, kill and destroy (John 10:10) and one of those things is our identity, so that we do not know who we are, which prevents us from living a life of purpose. However, there is good news, Christ came so that we may live a life of abundance (John 10:10), and that abundant life has to have a secure identity, a life of purpose and every good thing God has for us. So God will do whatever is necessary to ensure we know our identity, if we allow Him to, in order to partake in this life of abundance that is available for us. So cheers to no more living a lie and living a life of truth!

Prayer:

Father God, I thank You that in the midst of all our troubles, where our identities have been stolen, You are more than able to restore. Thank You that You love us so much to not leave us in our mess and still bring us out of the pit. Thank You that even when life circumstances and the effects of that tried to define me, You stepped in and redefined me. I pray that you give me the endurance to go through the process that is required for me to know who I am in Christ. I pray that I will begin to see myself as you see me and I pray I will begin to embrace and accept the real me from this day onwards. Amen!

CHAPTER 5

LOVED BACK TO LIFE

Healing, Freedom and Wholeness

Accepting God's unconditional love was pretty difficult for me to understand and receive. I didn't think it was possible to have a love so real and a love that I didn't have to earn. What I realised and learnt was that I needed to open my heart willingly to fully experience His love. It was then that I noticed a change and transformation in my life. Accepting His love for me was the first step into going on this path of healing, freedom and wholeness. Without the acceptance, I wouldn't be able to trust God to go to the depths of my heart to uproot all the things that caused issues and problems in my life. Though it has been a long ongoing process, it has been worth every single stage; I'm still on that road but I have come so far that I barely recognise myself because I have changed for the better and the real Seyi has finally emerged.

The same way there is a process in a wound healing, there is also a process the Lord takes us through when He takes us on the journey of healing in order to become totally free and whole internally. This process then starts to show forth externally, but by this stage, our character would have been changed, mind-sets renewed, identity restored and faith secured. It then propels one to confidently live the life of freedom that God has made available to us and live a life of purpose which God has predestined for us.

My heart was in a coma, as I would always describe when making reference to the old me. I was alive but dead on the inside, I felt and thought I was broken beyond repair and there was no hope. Encountering Jesus and surrendering my life to Him changed my story; my life was revived and my purpose was birthed.

> *Encountering Jesus and surrendering my life to Him changed my story; my life was revived and my purpose was birthed*

Whoever is reading this, let me encourage you to surrender your life to Him completely if you haven't already, it will be the best decision you have ever made and will be totally worth it. He loves you and He wants a relationship with you! Believe it or not; Jesus saves, I am a living witness and proof; if this was not the case you would not be reading this book!

Through this journey I had to make many decisions and change many things, to really have the full experience of this freedom. The Lord uprooted all the things that were not of Him; the things that bore fruit due to the things I went through: bitterness, pain, hurt, rejection, abandonment, homosexual tendencies, lust, sexual immorality, low self-esteem, anger, strife, jealously, fear, resentment and unforgiveness. As you can see, I was a total mess. I was full of so much junk but in His mercy, God poured His love into my heart and each of these things had to go because love and those could not mix, and I choose love.

I was intentional about being healed, seeing changes in my life, living a life that gave God glory in all things, pursuing holiness, righteousness and purpose. He began to change and transform me internally which started to become evident externally. My desires changed and His desires became my desires. Old habits had to go, I left the things of the world and its lifestyles (music, TV shows, inappropriate movies included) behind and relationships/friendships had to be cut off in order to embrace the new life God had for me. What I've learnt on this journey is that God didn't just care about healing and making me free, but He cared and still cares about every detail of my life and wants everything to be changed and reflect everything that He is. Intimacy with God is something He desires for me and you, God wants a relationship with His people. On this journey, having an intimate relationship with God has empowered and enabled me to follow through what He was/is doing in me, it ignited and still ignites the passion in my heart to read His word, to spend time with Him, hunger and thirst for righteousness, live a life of holiness, obedience and purpose. All that He needs is a willing heart; so are you willing to forsake everything to have Him, to get your healing, to live a life of freedom, to see changes in your life and become whole?

Staying free is the challenging part of the journey of wholeness but it is possible. It's only in Christ that you can do this because whom the Son sets free is free indeed (John 8:36). What you have read is a testimony of what God has done and can do. I share this not to tell a story, but to show you that there is hope; you are not too broken for God to fix because He

Staying free is the challenging part of the journey of wholeness but it is possible

is more than able to do what you can ever think or imagine (Ephesians 3:20).

I'm still on this journey, I am loving every moment of it even though sometimes it can be hard. I rest in the fact that His strength is made perfect in my weakness and it's so worth it. I am learning new things, I'm being moulded and transformed into His image, my character is being chiselled by Him, and I am being perfected in His love daily.

Don't think that everything you've been through has gone to waste

The beauty of this whole journey of healing, freedom and wholeness is not just that He loved me back to life, but that I am now able to do the same to many others too through Him. Don't think that everything you've been through has gone to waste; to your surprise that is the very thing He will use you to bring about freedom in others if you let Him. Isaiah 61 is what the Lord has done for me in my life and I am honoured and humbled that my purpose is linked to doing the same to those He has called me to.

Prayer:

Thank You God that it is Your heart's desire for us to be healed, free and be whole. Help us to endure the process that comes with the journey of healing, freedom and wholeness, and to allow patience to have its perfect way in us so that in the end we may be lacking in nothing. No matter what we have gone through, may this allow us to choose You, to draw near You, to receive and accept Your unconditional love and have a relationship with You, which will allow us to fulfil the plans You have for us that will ultimately declare nothing but Your glory. Amen!

CHAPTER 6

HOPE IN YOUR BROKENNESS

This chapter is to encourage you that whatever you are going through, there is hope in your brokenness. There are two main things I want to highlight here:

1. When your hope is deferred it can make your heart sick as the scripture Proverbs 13:12 says. When you do not see the light at the end of the tunnel, it just feels like there is no hope, but I want to encourage you that even in the midst of it all, when you look to God, that will change. Your hope that was once deferred will become a desire fulfilled.

2. Hope will not bring you shame or disappointment, so keep hoping. Don't be downcast and don't fear, but dare to hope and the fruits from that are those that money can never buy.

Hope Deferred to Desire Fulfilled

> *"Hope deferred makes the heart sick, but when the desire is fulfilled, it is a tree of life" (Proverbs 13:12, AMPC).*

The above scripture was one I have always heard here and there, something about it always stuck out to me but I didn't really have an understanding or deep revelation of what it actually meant. Only until I started writing this book, did I get the revelation of what this verse meant to me personally and I broke down in tears because this was my life. The first part of it was my reality until God's love came in and fulfilled my heart desires; the desire to be healed from pain, restored and made whole.

When we hope for things to get better in our lives and they don't get better it can really bring us to a dark place, it can make us feel depressed and utterly hopeless which then makes our heart sick. Sick of the disappointments, pain, brokenness, hopeless situations and circumstances we constantly have to battle with.

When God's love comes in, the desires of our heart are fulfilled. The desires of our heart actually change as we go through the healing process with God. His love makes us want the things He wants for our lives, the hopelessness becomes hope, the bondage becomes freedom, the things we have lost, He is able to restore double fold even if it's not in the same capacity as how it was lost. After all, He knows all things and knows what is good for us. He desires for us to be healed, to be free, restored and made whole and the tree of life is one that restoration and wholeness is a part of. The tree of life is God Himself because the tree of life is love.

When a desire is fulfilled, it is like a tree of life, which comes with so much good things from above. In essence, that desire which is fulfilled is one that is God's desire for us. As we allow Him to do a work in us, His desires become our desires. What is God's desire for us? Holiness, salvation (wholeness), righteousness, freedom, restoration, love, peace, joy, to name a few. So what am I trying to say? I'm saying when our hope is not deferred we allow LOVE in to make its perfect way in us.

Hope Will Not Bring Shame or Disappointment

Having hope is something you can have without anticipating shame or disappointment. I know this was one of my struggles when I fantasised about being happy one day. In the midst of all the chaos going on in my life, I dared to hope for a better future but something always took that vision away when doubt came in. As much as I desired for a better end than my beginning, I feared that it will just be a dream and not my reality. When I gave my life to Christ in 2012, things didn't all of a sudden change, but I felt different; it was a feeling I couldn't describe and that was enough to keep me hoping that one day things will surely get better. I came across Romans 5:3-5 and this really sparked something on the inside! It became more than a revelation and became my experience as the years went by; it gave me the confidence in what God was doing and the process He had me go through. Let's see what this passage says in the Amplified Version:

> "Moreover [let us also be full of joy now] let us exult and triumph in our troubles and rejoice in our sufferings, knowing that pressure and affliction and

hardship produce patience and unswerving endurance. And endurance (fortitude) develops maturity (approved faith and tried integrity). And character [of this sort] produces [the habit of] joyful and confident hope of eternal salvation. Such hope never disappoints or deludes or shames us, for God's love has been poured out in our hearts through the Holy Spirit Who has been given to us" (AMPC)

This is so encouraging to know; even in the difficult situations and times in our lives, there are benefits that will come out of it. Though it seems so hard to bear at times, the fruit of those sufferings is more valuable and useful to our future than we think. Imagine after all that, you mature in patience, unswerving endurance, character, experience which produces joy and confident hope. This hope is one of eternal salvation; let us look at what this confident hope of eternal salvation is. The root word of salvation is the Greek word *"sózó"* which translates to mean; *to heal, to save, to deliver and to be made whole.* So a better way to look at it when we are going through these things, is that when we allow God to help us through the process of enduring these tough times, at the end of it we get to a place where we can and will be healed, saved, delivered and made whole. Exciting isn't it? That certainly helps me see my trying times from a different perspective if I know that I will experience and be all those things

Dare to believe

after. And it doesn't just end there; this very hope will never shame or disappoint us. Once again, we have no reason not to hope now because the outcome is a safe one; it wouldn't make us feel any less than we are or allow us to think it can get any worse if we just dare to believe.

So why does this hope never disappoint or shame us? This is because it is God's love that has been poured into our hearts. God is love (1 John 4:8) and according to 1 Corinthians 13:8, love never fails. So hope in God can NEVER fail or disappoint us and we can confidently endure what we are going through and even look back and face the very things we found difficult to deal with and know that at the end of it we will be healed, saved, delivered and made whole.

What I went through made me who I am today. My past certainly doesn't define me but it surely contributed to who I am today; the good and the bad. I matured in patience, unswerving endurance, character and experience which gave me this habitual joy and confident hope in salvation. This can be you too, if you just have faith and endure, there is truly hope in your brokenness if you allow God to pour His love into your heart.

> *My past certainly doesn't define me but it surely contributed to who I am today*

The enemy comes to kill steal and destroy; he may have stolen, he may have killed but as long as you are breathing he hasn't yet destroyed meaning there is hope; hope to be restored, hope to come alive again and hope to face tomorrow.

Broken beyond repair was what I thought and concluded about my life. In my 2nd year of my Radiotherapy and Oncology degree, I had failed everything and the reality looked like one of no return. The 22-year-old girl was totally wrecked by everything that life had thrown at her and left her totally hopeless; 4 years later, she can tell you that there is hope in your brokenness despite what you have been through or are currently going through. These past few years have been a challenging but also beautiful journey; to

> **God can use our brokenness and make it His masterpiece**

look back and see who that 22-year-old girl was and now to see who this 26-year-old woman is, is enough evidence to justify that there is hope in your brokenness. God can use our brokenness and make it His masterpiece, He can make you something out of nothing and you are never too broken for God to fix.

Remember these truths:

The Lord is close to those who are of a broken heart and saves such as are crushed with sorrow for sin and are humbly and thoroughly penitent (Psalm 34:18, AMPC)

He heals the broken hearted and binds up their wounds [curing their pains and their sorrows] (Psalm 147:3, AMPC)

(He has come) to proclaim liberty to the [physical and spiritual] captives and open the prison and the eyes of those that are bound (Isaiah 61:1, AMPC, brackets mine)

He has come to grant consolation and joy to those who mourn, to give them beauty for ashes, the oil of joy instead of mourning, the garment of praise instead of a heavy, burdened and failing spirit that He may be glorified (Isaiah 61:3). So be patient, for surely there is an end and your expectation/hope shall not be cut off (Proverbs 23:18), for in this hope we were saved.

But hope which is seen is not hope, for how can one hope for what he already sees? But If we hope for what is still unseen by us, we wait for it with patience and composure (Romans 8:24-25, AMPC).

Prayer:

Lord I thank You that there is hope in my brokenness, thank You that Your Word reminds me that You are close to the broken hearted and You bind up their wounds. Lord I pray that I would allow You to pour Your love into my heart so that I can confidently hope and never be disappointed or ashamed of what my future will hold in You. Help me not to defer hope any longer so that my heart desires will be fulfilled according to your will. I declare and decree total healing in my spirit, mind and soul, restoration and wholeness for the rest of my life from this day henceforth. Amen!

CHAPTER 7

ENCOURAGING SCRIPTUR

This *"Healing and restoration is made available, a price that has been paid and can never be replaceable. Christ is willing to make you whole; binding up the wounds of your broken soul"*

Above is a line from a poem I wrote last year. You don't have to do this on your own, the ways of the world will never give you the answers and love you are looking for, I tried it and it failed me big time. There is Someone available Who can fill all the voids that need filling in your life, Who can bind up your wounds, Who can give you hope, Who can love you like no other... Jesus Christ, the Way, the Truth and the Life (John 14:6)!

Here are some scriptures to meditate on and to make reference to in times of need; times when you don't feel like you can carry on, times when your situation or

.stances seem too much to bear and times when you
.eel like there is no hope. Sometimes you just need to be
reminded and encouraged that there is hope, even when it
does not seem like there is. Hope in Christ is secure, it is
sure and it is real. Pray fervently, let go, surrender all, cling
on to Jesus, depend, trust and rely on Him, He is faithful
and surely He will never leave nor forsake you!

*"Come to Me, all you who labour and are heavy laden, and I
will give you rest. Take My yoke upon you and learn from
Me, for I am gentle and lowly in heart, and you will find rest
for your souls. For My yoke is easy and My burden is light"*
(Matthew 11:28-30, NKJV)

*"The Lord is near to those who have a broken heart, and
saves such as have a contrite spirit" (Psalm 34:18, NKJV)*

"Be anxious for nothing, but in everything by prayer and supplication, with thanksgiving, let your requests be known to God; and the peace of God, which surpasses all understanding, will guard your hearts and mind through Christ Jesus" (Philippians 4:6-7, NKJV)

"When my father and my mother forsake me, then the Lord will take care of me" (Psalm 27:10, NKJV)

"The Lord is my shepherd; I shall not want, He makes me lie down in green pastures, He leads me beside still waters. He restores my soul, He leads me in the path of righteousness for His name's sake" (Psalm 23:1-3, NKJV)

"There is no fear in love; but perfect love casts out fear, because fear involves torment. But he who fears has not been made perfect in love" (1 John 4:18, NKJV)

"Therefore if the Son makes you free, you shall be free indeed" (John 8:36, NKJV)

"Arise [from the depression and prostration in which circumstances have kept you – rise to a new life]! Shine (be radiant with the glory of the Lord), for your light has come, and the glory of the Lord has risen upon you!" (Isaiah 60:1, AMPC)

"I can do all things through Christ who strengthens me" (Philippians 4:13, NKJV)

"There is therefore now no condemnation to those who are in Christ Jesus, who do not walk according to the flesh but according to the Spirit" (Romans 8:1, NKJV)

"What then shall we say to these things? If God is for us, who can be against us?" (Romans 8:31, NKJV)

"Who shall separate us from the love of Christ? Shall tribulation, or distress, or persecution, or famine, or nakedness, or peril, or sword? As it is written: "For Your sake we are killed all day long; we are accounted as sheep for the slaughter". Yet in all these things we are more than conquerors through Him who loved us. For I am persuaded that neither death nor life, nor angels nor principalities nor powers, nor things present nor things to come, nor height nor depth, nor any created thing, shall be able to separate us from the love of God which is in Christ Jesus our Lord".
(Romans 8:35 – 39, NKJV)

"Therefore, if anyone is in Christ, he is a new creation, old things have passed away; behold, all things have become new" *(2 Corinthians 5:17, NKJV)*

"For the weapons of our warfare are not carnal but mighty in God for pulling down strongholds, casting down arguments and every high thing that exalts itself against the knowledge of God, bringing every thought into captivity to the obedience of Christ, and being ready to punish all disobedience when your obedience is fulfilled" *(2 Corinthians 10:4-6, NKJV)*

"And do not be conformed to this world, but be transformed by the renewing of your mind, that you may prove what is that good and acceptable and perfect will of God" *(Romans 12:2, NKJV)*

"Just as He chose us in Him before the foundation of the world, that we should be holy and without blame before Him in love, having predestined us to adoption as sons by Jesus Christ to Himself, according to the good pleasures of His will, to the praise of the glory of His grace, by which He made us accepted in the Beloved" (Ephesians 1:4-6, NKJV)

"For God has not given us a spirit of fear, but of power and of love and of a sound mind" (2 Timothy 1:7, NKJV)

"But let patience have its perfect work, that you may be perfect and complete, lacking nothing" (James 1:4, NKJV)

"Every good gift and perfect gift is from above, and comes down from the Father of lights, with whom there is no variation or shadow of turning" (James 1:17, NKJV)

"Draw near to God and He will draw near to you"
(James 4:8, NKJV)

"Beloved, do not think it strange concerning the fiery trial which is to try, as some strange thing happen to you; but rejoice to the extent that you partake of Christ sufferings, that when His glory is revealed, you may also be glad with exceeding joy" (1Peter 4:12-13, NKJV)

"Casting all your care upon Him, for He cares for you"
(1 Peter 5:7, NKJV)

"This hope we have as an anchor of the soul, both sure and steadfast" (Hebrews 6:19a, NKJV)

"But thanks be to God, who gives us the victory through our Lord Jesus Christ. Therefore, my beloved brethren, be steadfast, immovable, always abounding in the work of the Lord, knowing that your labour is not in vain in the Lord" (1 Corinthians 15:57-58, NKJV)

"The Lord takes pleasure in those who fear Him, in those who Hope in His mercy" (Psalm 147:11, NKJV)

"For I know the thoughts that I think towards you, says the Lord, thoughts of peace and not of evil, to give you a future and a hope" (Jeremiah 29:11, NKJV)

"But as it is written "Eye has not seen, nor ear heard, nor have entered into the heart of man the things which God has prepared for those who love Him"
(1 Corinthians 2:9, NKJV)

"Rejoicing in hope, patient in tribulation, continuing steadfastly in prayer" (Romans 12:12, NKJV)

"Now may the God of hope fill you with all joy and peace in believing, that you may abound in hope by the power of the Holy Spirit" (Romans 15:13, NKJV)

"Be strong and of good courage, do not fear nor be afraid of them; for the Lord your God, He is the One who goes with you. He will not leave you nor forsake you"
(Deuteronomy 31:6, NKJV)

"But those who wait on the Lord shall renew their strength; they shall mount up with wings like eagles, they shall run and not be weary, they shall walk and not faint"
(Isaiah 40:31, NKJV)

"For we were saved in this hope, but hope that is seen is not hope; for why does one still hope for what he sees?"
(Romans 8:24, NKJV)

"For surely there is a hereafter, and your hope will not be cut of" (Proverbs 23:18, NKJV)

"Blessed is the man who trusts in the Lord and whose hope is the Lord" (Jeremiah 17:7, NKJV)

"But I will hope continually, and will praise You yet more and more" (Psalm 71:14, NKJV)

"Fear not, for I am with you; be not dismayed, for I am your God. I will strengthen you, yes I will help you, I will uphold you with My righteous right hand" (Isaiah 41:10, NKJV)

"Jesus said to him, if you can believe, all things are possible to him who believes" (Mark 9:23, NKJV)

"But seek first the kingdom of God and His righteousness, and all these things shall be added to you" (Matthew 6:33, NKJV).

ABOUT THE AUTHOR

Seyi is a living testimony of an overcomer chosen to share the message of hope to those that are hopeless, just like  she once was. She is passionate about seeing people move forward from the very thing that has kept them bound and embraces the journey of healing, restoration and wholeness the Lord had her on when she had lost hope. Receiving and experiencing God's unconditional love propels her to share and extend His love to others and bring them to the knowledge of who He is with compassion, which ultimately brings about restoration eternally. Seyi is the founder of Divine Epiphany; a woman's organisation and works in the city of London, United Kingdom, as a qualified Therapeutic Radiographer (Radiotherapist).

Made in the USA
Charleston, SC
27 July 2016